A Quiet Pint in Kinvara

By RICHARD TILLINGHAST

Drawings by ANNE KORFF

Salmon Publishing
and
Tír Eolas, Guide & Map Publishers

© Richard Tillinghast, 1991
© Anne Korff, 1991

Typeset and printed by Nova Print, Galway

ISBN 0948339 63 2   £3.95

We acknowledge the help of Galway County
Council with this publication.

Salmon Publishing   Tír Eolas
Bridge Mills   Newtownlynch
Galway   Kinvara, Co. Galway
Ireland   Ireland

Foreword

I first met Richard Tillinghast having a quiet pint in Kinvara. In The Ould Plaid Shawl, to be precise. A friend of mine, who had already met Richard, had been trying to bring us together for a while, but somehow we kept missing each other. How and why friendships begin is a mysterious business, but as we talked that Sunday afternoon, our tongues loosened by several glasses of Arthur Guinness's finest, I realised we two Americans - he here for a year and myself for well over twenty - had a number of things in common.

One of these things is Kinvara. Over the past decade I have immersed myself in the history of this particular part of South Galway. Richard, like myself, is another example of someone who has fallen under the strong enchantment of Kinvara and the potent atmosphere of the West of Ireland. And it is this he celebrates in his fine poem.

Buildings make a statement in the face of wild nature. Buffeted by strong westerly winds, soaked on a regular basis by the rain the farmer both greets as a friend and fears as an enemy, over the centuries Kinvara people - country people, priests, merchants, Gaelic chieftains, landlords - have, as Richard puts it, extended "a fleshy hand, palm outward, against the sea, saying Land starts Here. Go peddle your salt airs elsewhere".

In his poem Richard Tillinghast has brought a sharpened sensitivity to this particular village - special and yet typical - and through his eyes all of us can now see a little more clearly what defines Kinvara as the unique place it is, for both the "stranger" and the native. As a "blow-in" who has put down his own roots here, I am very grateful for the stroke of chance or destiny that brought him here.

Jeff O'Connell

Salt-stung, rain-cleared air, deepened as always
By a smudge of turf smoke. Overhead the white glide
Of seagulls, and in the convent beeches above the road,
Hoarse croak of rooks, throaty chatter of jackdaws.
High tide pounds stone wall.
I shut my door behind me and head downhill,

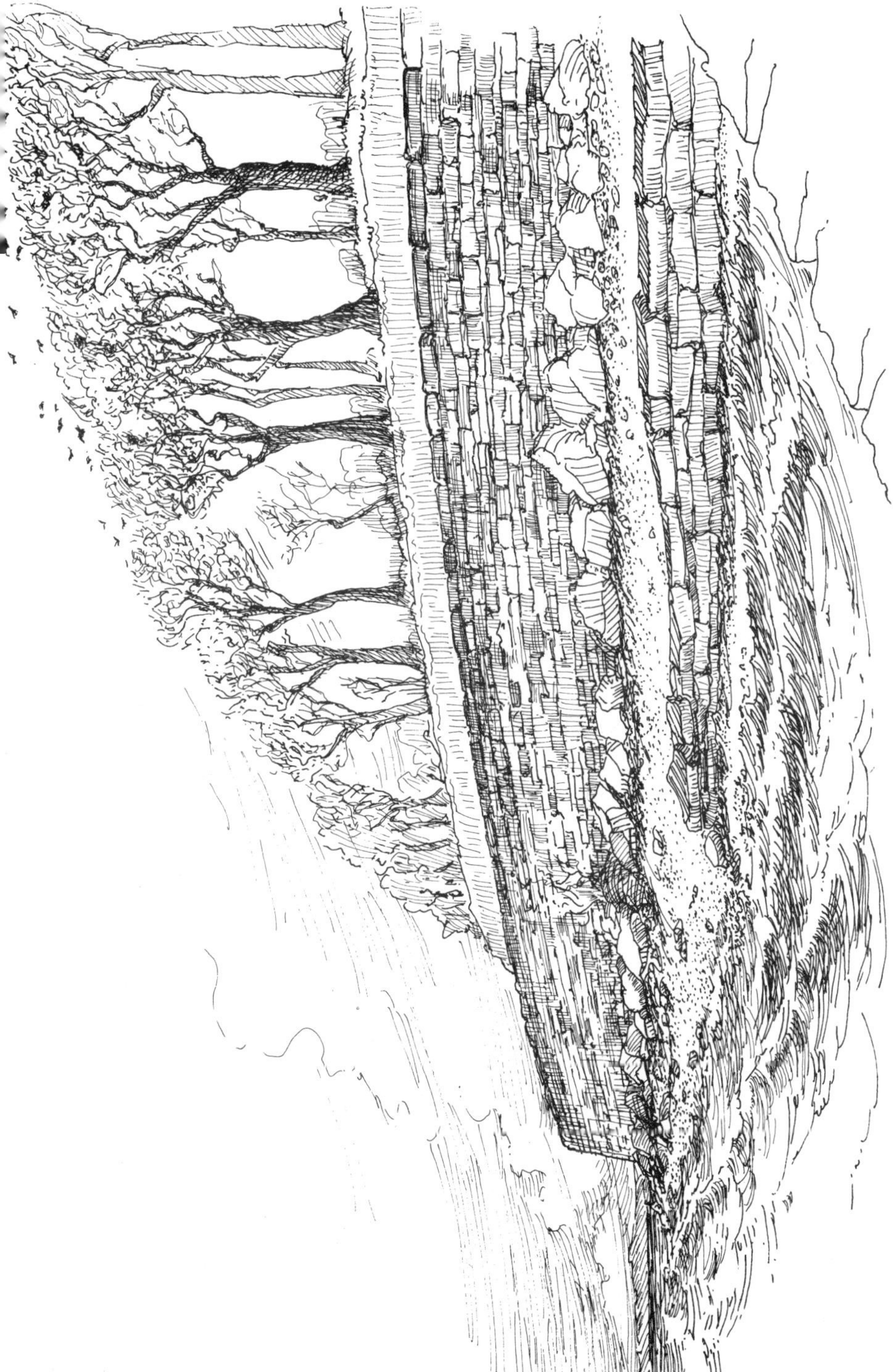

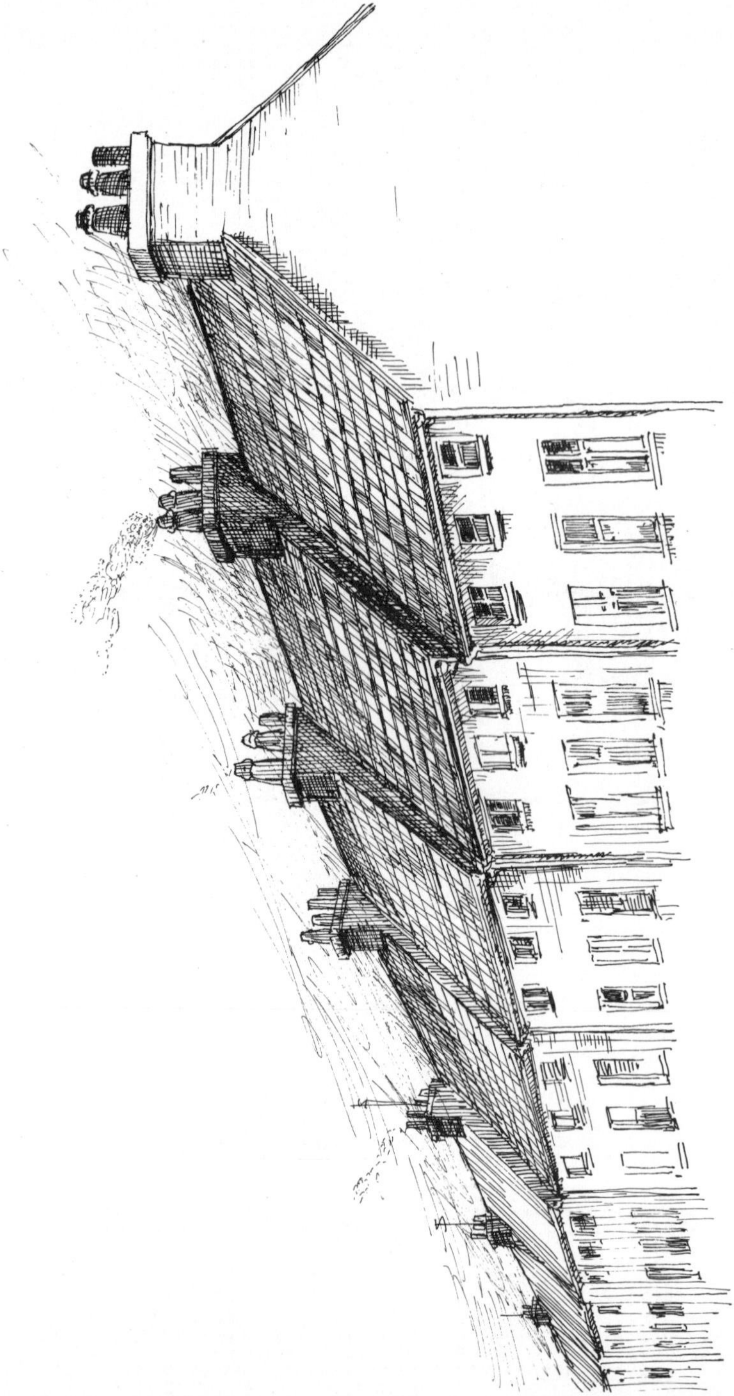

Gait steadied by the broad-shouldered gravity
Of houses from the eighteenth or nineteenth century —

Limestone, three storeys, their slate roofs rain-slick,

Aglow with creeper and the green brilliance of mosses.

No force off the Atlantic

Could threaten their angles or budge their masses.

They rise unhurriedly from the strong cellar
And hold a fleshy hand, palm outward, against the sea,
Saying "Land starts here. Go peddle your salt airs elsewhere."
From farms down lanes the meat and milk of pasture,
Root crops and loads of hay,
By hoof or wagon, come down to Kinvara quay.

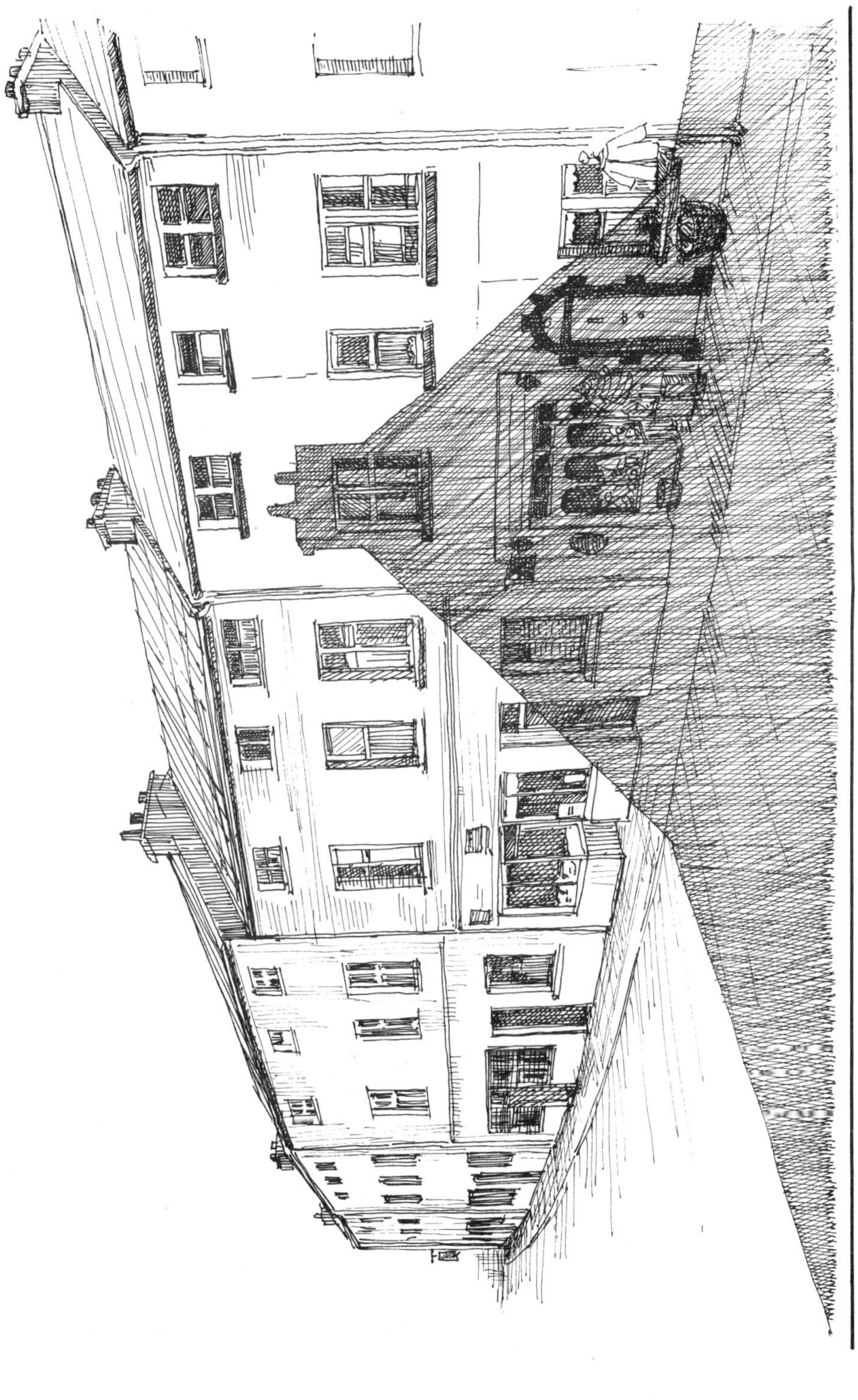

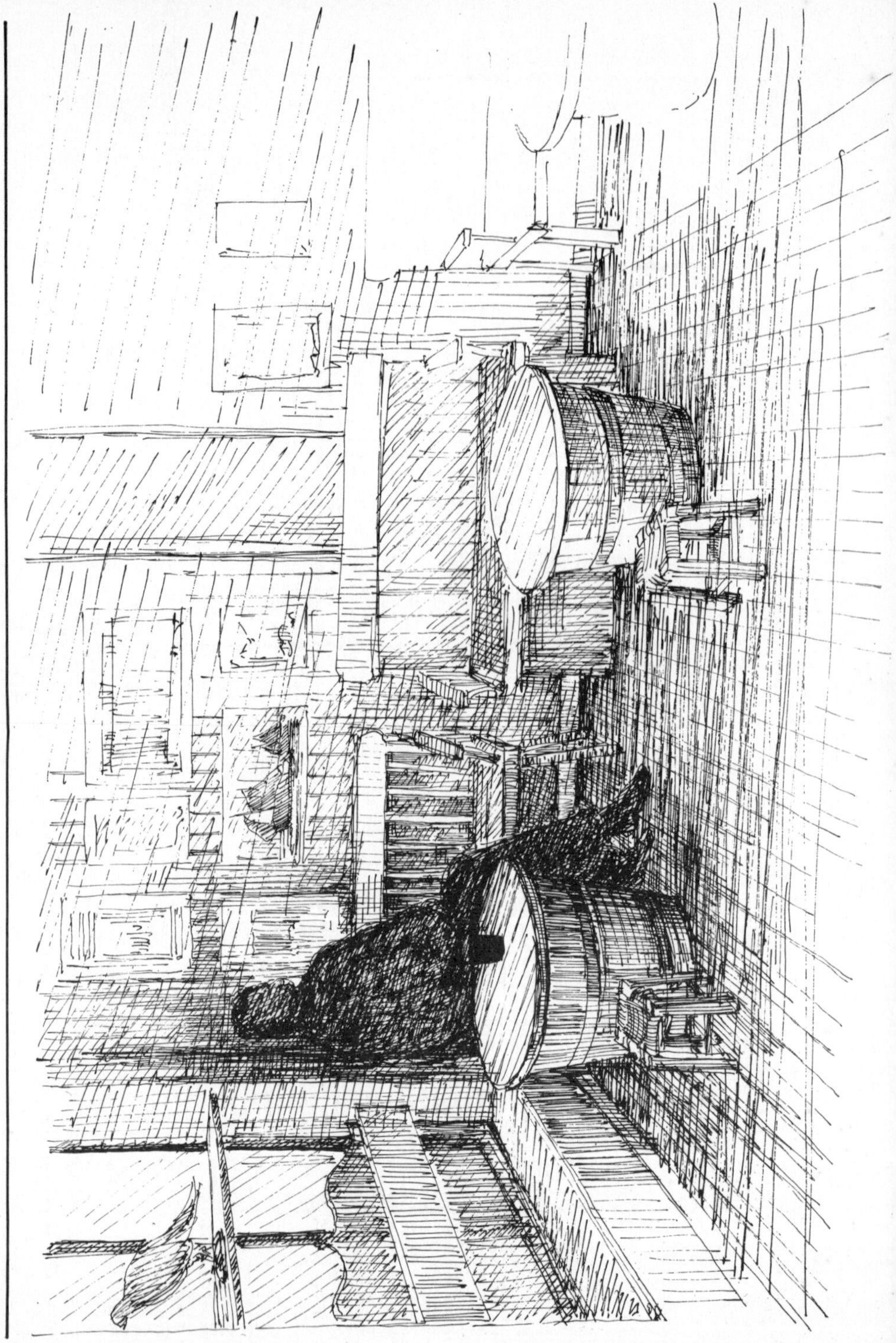

A nd so do I—to drink in the presence

Of these presences, these ideas given substance,

Solid as your father's signature

On a letter you unfold sometimes from a quiet drawer,

Yet semi-detached, half free,

Like the road that follows the sea down from Galway,

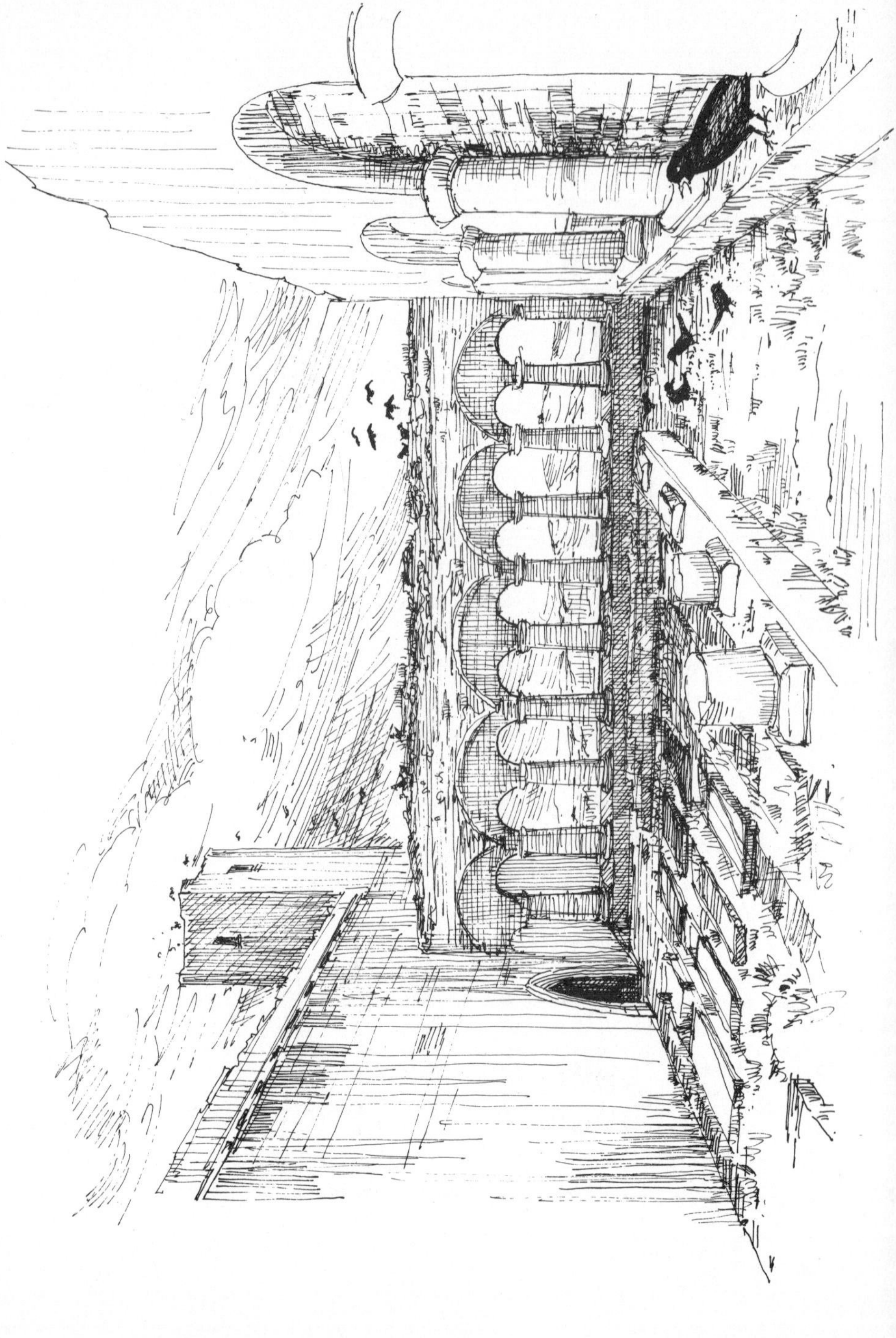

Curving like a decorated S
Drizzled through a monk's quill plucked from the goose,
Spelling *Sanctus* onto vellum newly missed by the herd,
In a cell where the soul's damp candle flared—
Roofless now to the weather's
Inundations, while ravens walk the cloisters.

Gloria of martyrdom, kingship's crimson
Are shattered now, buried in mire. The mizzling sky
Darkens unmitigated over thatch collapsed into famine,
Tracks leading nowhere. Absences occupy
The four kingdoms. A wide-eyed
Angel stares uncomprehendingly skyward,

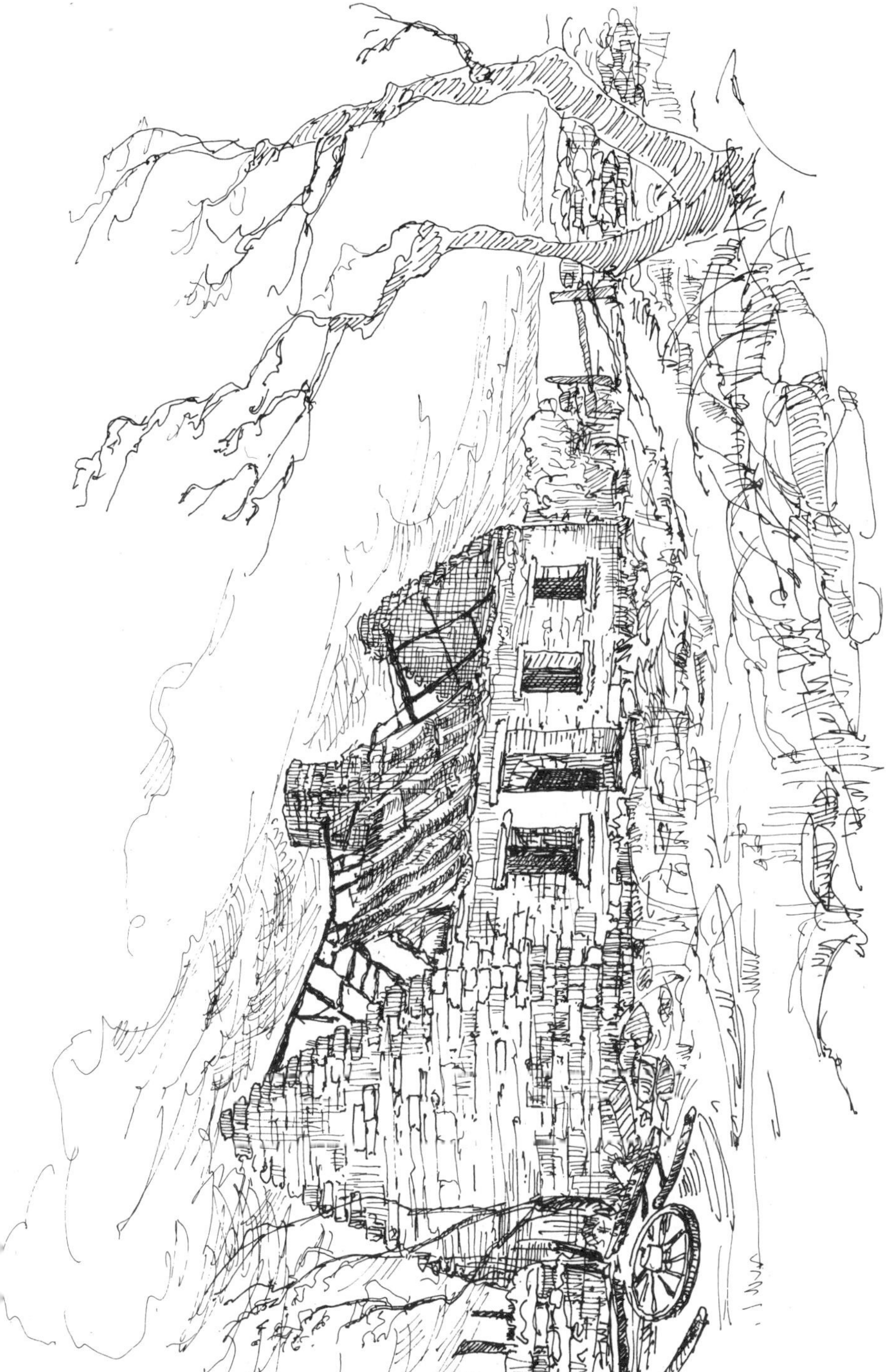

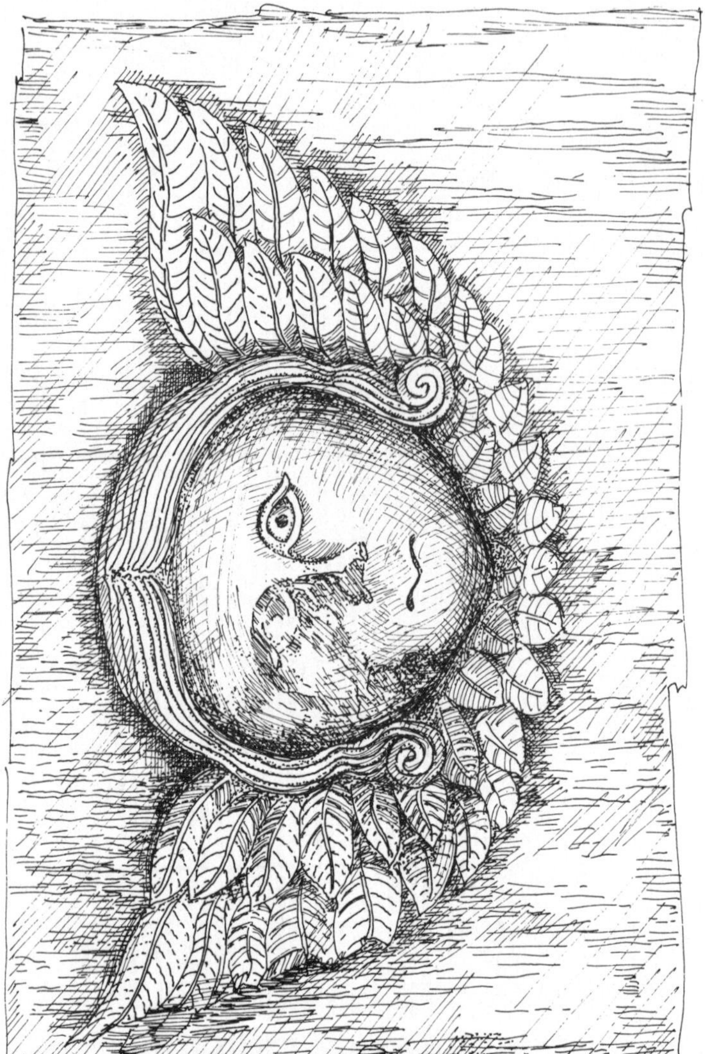

Stone angel of the Island, baptised by rain,
Outlasting Viking longboat, Norman strongbow,

Face battered by a rifle butt.   Tough-minded as a bloody saint.

But where was I off to, mind like a darkened window

This dampened afternoon?

To the pub of course.   It's time for that quiet pint,

Brewed blacker than ruination, sound

As fresh-hewn timber, strong as a stonecutter's hand.

Make it stout like the roof overhead, to take off the chill

That blows through emptied fields. Let me drink my fill

And more, of that architecture –

Then ease home tight and respectable to dinner.

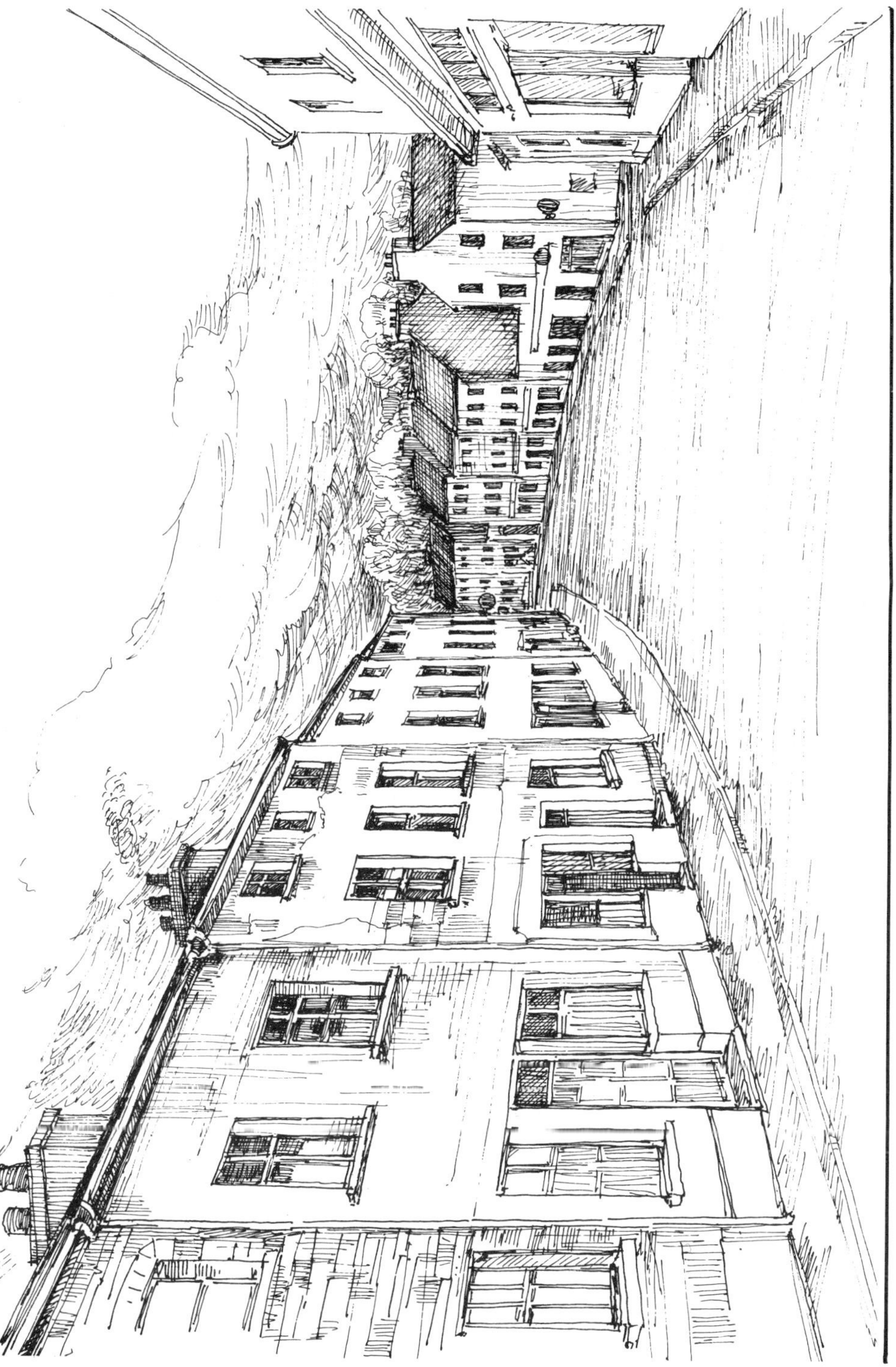